Antibacterial and phytochemical activity of *Justicia adhatoda*: an overview

Prem Jose Vazhacharickal, John Joseph, Sukanya N. S and Christy Joy

Table of contents

Table of figures

Table of tables

List of abbreviations

mg	: Milligram
mm	: Millimeter
°C	: Degree celcius
µg	: Microgram
MR	: Methyl red
VP	: Voges-Proskauer
TSI	: Triple sugar iron
H_2O_2	: Hydrogen peroxide

Antibacterial and phytochemical activity of *Justicia adhatoda*: an overview

Prem Jose Vazhacharickal[1]*, John Joseph[2], Sukanya N. S[2] and Christy Joy[2]
* premjosev@gmail.com
[1]Department of Biotechnology, Mar Augusthinose College, Ramapuram, Kerala, India-686576

[2]Department of Bioscience, Indira Gandhi College of Arts and Science, Nellikuzhi, Kerala, India-686691

Abstract

Justicia adhatoda is a natural plant with lot of medicinal properties. To evaluate the strength of antimicrobial effectiveness of the ethanolic extract of *Justica adhatoda*, Muller-Hinton agar was used as the base medium for screening of antibacterial activity and antibiotic sensitivity test. Four bacterial strains are used; *Escherichia coli*, Klebsiella species, Pseudomonas species, *Staphylococcus aureus*. Antibiotic sensitivity is based on disc diffusion method. The Pseudomonas species shows higher activity. It is a multi-drug resistance in human and animal pathogenic bacteria. This is less expensive, safe and an effective natural extract.

Keywords: *Justica adhatoda*, Biochemical characterization, *E.coli*, *Staphylococcus aureus*.

1. Introduction

Ayurveda is commonly known as the science of longevity and it is oldest and available method of treatment in India. Ayu means life; Veda means knowledge. Ayurveda is a combination of the soul, mind and the body. Ayurvedic concepts appeared and developed between 2,500 and 500 BC in India. The literal meaning of Ayurveda is "Science of life', because ancient Indian system of health care focused views of man and his illness. It is pointed out that the positive health means metabolically well balanced human beings. According to Ayurveda, the disease evolves from the body due to external factors. It has a vast literature in Sanskrit covering all aspect of diseases, pharmacy and therapeutics. Its main aim is the preservation for normal persons and treatment of sick individuals using only natural methods.

Charka, Sushrutha, Vagbhata, Madhava and Sharangadhara were the great Acharya or scholars of ayurvedic medicines. They had great power of observation, generalization and analysis.

The principles of ayurvedic treatment are same as that of allopathic treatment. They consist of removing the injurious agent, soothing injured body and mind and eradicating the cause. The difference lies in the methods of detail adopted by the different systems. In Ayurveda great importance is given upon the study of various stages of vitiation of the three Doshas.

[Note: The three Doshas are - Vatha (wind), Pitta (bile) and Kapha (phlegm). The seven Dhatus are – Rasa (chyle), Raktha (blood), Mamsa (flesh), Medas (fat), Asthi (bone), Majja (marrow) and Shukla (sperm). The three Malas are –sweat, urine and excreta.]

Disease, according to Ayurveda, is generally defined as derangement of the three Doshas. Health is an equilibrium of the three Doshas. Ayurveda is the science of life. It shows the way to remove diseases, to keep up health and attain longevity.

Medicinal plants which form the backbone of traditional medicine have in the last few decades been the subject of very intense pharmacological studies. This has been brought about by the acknowledgement of the value of medicinal plant as potential source of new compounds of therapeutic value and as a source of new compounds in drug development. In many parts of the world medicinal plants are used for antibacterial, antifungal and antiviral activities.

1.1 *Justicia adhatoda* (adalodakam)

Justicia adhatoda Linn. belongs to family Acanthaceae, is a Diffuse shrubs. Leaves ovate or elliptics- lanceolate, acuminate, up to 20 cm long. Flowers are white, streaked with pink or purple. Spikes pedunculate clustered towards branch end. Bract large, leafy, ovate, glabrous, 6 -7 nerved, bracteoles 1- nerved. Corolla tube short upper tip galeate, subentir, lower spreading and 3- lobed. Stamens 2 inserted near the mouth of corolla tube; filaments hairy near base. The fruit is a legume, 30–60 cm (12–23 in) long and 1.5–2.5 cm (0.5–1 in) broad, with a pungent odour. Seeds are Sub-orbicular, rugose. It is found throughout India ascending to 4,000 ft, elevation, in sub- Himalayan tracts and commonly in the plains. It is 1.5-2 meter tall shrub. Its leaves are ovate or elliptics- lanceolate, acuminate, up to 20 cm long. *Justicia adhatoda* Linn. is mentioned as vasa in Ayurvedic classics and has been used in various dosage forms to treat asthma, cough, wound ulcer, fever and cough. The leaves are bitter in taste.

The leaves extract has been reported to contain polysaccharide, proteins, uronic acids, saponins, tannins, triterpenes, alkaloids, and flavonoids, essential oils having antitussive, wound healing and antimicrobial activity. The leaves have been reported to contain alkaloids, vasicinone, vasicinol, adhatodine, adhatonine, adhavasinone, anisotine and peganine as major constituents. The leaves has been reported to possess antibacterial, wound healing, antitubercular, immunomodulator, antitussive properties. Authenticity, purity and assay are the three major attributes for standardization and quality control. Hence, in this work we just made an attempt for the standardization of *Justicia adhatoda* Linn. by carrying out its pharmacognostic evaluation.

It is widely used for its general healing and strengthening properties in Ayurveda. This plant is identifiable with its peculiar red color with a black spot on a side. Powdered seeds also are believed to prevent conception in women.

Leaves are the main useable part. The leaves form a part of special food preparations for nursing women. It is also a mild laxative and purgative. It has a sedative properties too. Its leaves are rich in vitamin C. There are different alkaloids present in adalodakam. It is a part of many ayurvedic medicines.

People use herbs to treat different diseases because they are cheap and effective, but doctors are often reluctant to prescribe them because of knowledge deficiency, real concerns about product safety, concerns about liability, and the presence of pathogens and compounds that are injurious. Medicinal plants are very important for the cure of different microbial infections but heavy metals adversely affect bacterial viability and activity. Experiments on the use of plant compounds against microbes were first documented in the late 19th century. Natural products perform various functions and many have interesting and useful biological activities. Researchers are turning their attention to natural products to develop better anticancer, antiviral and antibacterial drugs. Antimicrobial properties of medicinal plants are being increasingly reported from different parts of the world. Many researchers have examined the uses of medicinal plants, but only a few studies have tested these Ethno-botanical findings in a laboratory setting to confirm the real antimicrobial properties of these plants.

Medicinal plants can provide a wealth of antimicrobial agents, and hundreds have been investigated for biological activities. Local people collect raw materials in small quantities and use them to treat diseases. Raw materials are also collected in huge amounts and traded in the marketplace to supply herbal industries. Pathogens and parasites will remain the greatest threat to humans. Climate change may allow pathogens to establish in new areas.

1.2 Taxonomy of *Justicia adhatoda*

Kingdom: Plantae-- planta, plantes, plants, vegetal

Subkingdom: Viridiplantae

Superdivision: Embryophyta

Division: Tracheophyta

Class: Magnoliopsida

Order: Lamiales

Family: Acanthaceae

Genus: Justicia L.

Species: *Justicia adhatoda* L.

1.3 Aim

The aim of this study is to evaluate the antimicrobial and phytochemical activity of *Justicia adhatoda* against microorganism isolated from cough samples.

1.4 Objectives

The objectives of the current research work are to characterize and evaluate the phytochemical and antimicrobial activity of *Justicia adhatoda* against various microorganisms causing cough.

2. Review of literature

Justicia adhatoda is a well-known plant drug in Ayurvedic and Unani medicines (Claeson et al., 2000). It is used by Ayurvedic physicians and possesses some medicinal properties. It has been used for the treatment of various diseases and disorders, particularly for the respiratory tract ailments. Therefore, it is a primary herb of the Ayurvedic system used in the treatment of cough, bronchitis, asthma and symptoms of common cold (Karthikeyan et al., 2009). The source of the drug 'Vasaka' is well known in the indigenous system of medicine for its beneficial effects, particularly in bronchitis (Kumar et al., 2005). Similarly Bisolven, a branded drug containing Vasaka as an ingredient is used to clear the airways by decreasing the mucus secretions and opening the passages (Racle, 1976).

There are various herbal formulations accessible for the treatment of various kinds of respiratory disorders. Such as, Kanjang, an oral solution with a fixed combination of standardized extracts of *Echinacea purpurea*, *Justicia adhatoda* and *Eleutherococeus senticosus* has been used in the relief of symptoms allied with the common cold (coughing and irritability of the throat), with a well-established medical use comprising 50 million human daily doses (Narimanian et al., 2005). The major efficacy of this solution is mainly due to the presence of Vasaka. Other constituents of Kanjang have been exposed to have anti- stress effects, which might be occasioned partly by an endocrine and partly by an immunomodulatory mechanism of action.

This plant is a source of Vitamin C and has medicinal uses, mainly fever reducer, anti-inflammatory, anti-bleeding, bronchodilator, anti-diabetic, disinfectant, anti-jaundice and oxytoxic (Maurya and Singh, 2010). It is antiperiodic, astringent, diuretic, purgative and is also used as an expectorant in addition to liquefy sputum (Salalamp et al., 1996). The leaves, flowers and roots of this plant used in herbal drugs against tubercular activities (Barry et al., 1955), cancer (Pandey, 2002) and possessed anti-helminthic properties (Ayyanar and Ignacimuthu, 2008). The leaf juice is stated to cure diarrhoea, dysentery and glandular tumour (Ayyanar and cough, pneumonia, fever, jaundice, catarrh, whooping cough and asthma (Asolkar et al., 1992).

All the parts of *Justicia adhatoda* has been used for their curative effects from ancient times (Atal, 1980). It has been used in Ayurvedic system of medicine for the treatment of various ailments of respiratory tract in both children and adults. Various parts of the plant are used in Indian traditional medicine for the treatment of asthma, joint pain, lumber pain, sprains, cold, cough, eczema, malaria, rheumatism, swelling and venereal diseases (Jain, 1991). *Justicia adhatoda* has also been used by the European medical practitioners. The fluid extract and tincture were used in England as an Antispasmodic, Expectorant and febrifuge. It was said to be beneficial in intermittent, typhus fever and Diphtheria (Wren, 1932). In Germany, the leaves are used as an expectorant and spasmolytic agent (Madaus, 1938). In Sweden *Justicia adhatoda* is classified as a natural remedy and some preparations against cough containing an extract of Vasaka are accessible (Farnlof, 1998). The ethnomedicinal uses of various parts of *Justicia adhatoda* are along these lines.

The whole plant is used as an ingredient of numerous popular formulations including cough syrup used in combination with Ginger (*Zingiber officinale*) and Tulsi (*Ocimum sanctum*) where it exerts its action as an expectorant and antispasmodic (Atal, 1980). The plant is used for treatment of excessive phlegm and menorrhagia in Sri Lanka (Kirtikar and Basu, 1975). It is also used for the treatment of bleeding piles (Ahmad et al., 2009) and sexual disorders (Pushpangadan et al., 1995).

A yogic practice is to chew the leaf buds alone or with a little ginger root, to clear the respiratory passages in preparation for the vigorous breathing exercises. The various preparation of leaves are used for curing bleeding, haemorrhage, skin diseases, wounds, headache and leprosy in Southeast Asia (Adnan et al., 2010; Atta-Ur-Rahman et al., 1986; Roberts, 1931). The bruised fresh leaves are used for snake-bites in India and Sri Lanka (Roberts, 1931). Usually, yellow leaves are exploited for cough (Lal and Yadav, 1983) and smoke from leaves is used for asthma (Shah and Joshi, 1971). The plant leaves are used for checking postpartum haemorrhage and urinary trouble (Pushpangadan et al.,1995). It is found that 70% of the pregnant women in the Gora village of Lucknow (Uttar Pradesh, India) use the leaves of *Justicia adhatoda* to induce abortion (Nath et al., 1997). Moreover, it is observed that the Neterhat people in Bihar (India) used a decoction of the leaves to stimulate and heal before and after delivery (Jain et al., 1994). The leaf powder boiled in same oil is used to stop bleeding, earaches as well as pus from ears (Reddy et al., 1989) and jaundice

(Reddy et al., 1988). Decoction and ash of leaves are used for bronchial complaints such as asthma, tuberculosis (Jain and Puri, 1984), antipyretic (Jain, 1965) and relieve acidity. The leaves are toxic to 'all forms of lower life' and have insecticidal effects (Agrawal et al., 1986). It was also used for stomach catarrh with constipation, gout, urinary stone (Madaus, 1938) and warmed leaves used externally for rheumatic pains and dislocation of joint (Rao and Jamir, 1982). Moreover, the preparation of leaves in spirit is used for curing the wealthy persons suffering from certain humours in Myanmar (Kirtikar and Basu, 1975).

In the present study, the antimicrobial activity of methanolic extract of *Justicia adhatoda* was determined against Gram positive, Gram negative pathogenic bacteria and fungi along with pure vasicine and reference antibiotics.

Staphylococcus aureus is gram positive cocci that occur in grape like structure. First observed in human pyogenic lesions by von Recklinghhausen in 1891. It causes a variety of suppurative infections.

Escherichia coli and Klebsiella are the organisms included in the coli forms that are natural flora of the colon. But express pathogenicity and toxins.

Pseudomonas aeruginosa is a large group of gram negative bacillus. A few causes human infection, typically opportunistic. It causes urinary tract infections, respiratory tract infections, bacteraemia, bone and joint infections and gastrointestinal infections.

3. Hypothesis

The current research work is based on the following hypothesis

1) The extracts of *Justicia adhatoda* possess antibacterial and phytochemical activity.

4. Materials and Methods

4.1 Study area

Kerala state covers an area of 38,863 km^2 with a population density of 859 per km^2 and spread across 14 districts. The climate is characterized by tropical wet and dry with average annual rainfall amounts to 2,817 ± 406 mm and mean annual temperature is 26.8°C (averages from 1871-2005; Krishnakumar et al., 2009). Maximum rainfall occurs from June to September mainly due to South West Monsoon and temperatures are highest in May and November.

4.2 Collection and processing of samples

In this study, cough samples were collected from a clinical laboratory. The samples were observed directly with naked eye to check the nature of the specimen. Later the samples were gram stained to observe the presence of pus cells, epithelial cells and microorganisms. The organisms were characterized using nutrient agar, MacConkey agar and blood agar.

4.3 Isolation of pathogens

Cough samples were collected for the isolation of suspected organism. The samples were directly inoculated into Nutrient agar, MacConkey agar and Blood agar plates. Incubate the plates at 37°C for 24 hours. After incubation colonies were selected to study their morphological characters and identification procedures are carried out.

4.4 Identification of the pathogens
4.4.1 Colony characteristics

After incubation colony characteristics of the typical isolated colonies were studied. Colony characteristics such as size, forms, margin and elevation, opacity, consistency, pigmentation, lactose fermentation and haemolysis were studied.

4.4.2 Gram staining

i.   Smear of the isolates are prepared in a clean slide
ii. It is air dried and heat fixed
iii. The smear is flooded with crystal violet for 1 minute and then washed away with water
iv. Then smear is flooded with Gram's iodine for 1 minute
v.   Then it is washed away with decolourising agent such as 95% alcohol or acetone and washed with water
vi. Flood the smear with counter stain safranin and kept for 45 seconds and then wash with water
vii. The smear is air dried and observe under oil immersion objective.

4.4.3 Motility

i.   Apply Vaseline or parafilm wax at the edge of the cover slip
ii. Using a clean loop aseptically transfer a loopful of culture on cover slip
iii. Invert the cavity slide over the cover slip and press down to make firm seal
iv. Quickly and carefully turn down the slide so that drop is suspended into cavity
v.   Examine drop by first locating edge of drop by focusing it under the low power objective

vi. Reduce the light to see the edges as bright waxy line against grey background. Turn to high power and focus the edge of the drop to see motile and non-motile bacteria at the edge of the drop

4.5 Biochemical characterization
4.5.1 Sugar fermentation

i. Prepare sugar solution (sterile 1% sugar in 2% peptone water base with bromocresol purple indicator and inverted Durham's tube)
ii. Use a sterile Pasteur pipette to inoculate the medium
iii. Alternatively the medium can be inoculated with a charged wire loop
iv. After inoculation, tubes were incubated overnight.

4.5.2 Indole production-Kovac's method

i. Peptone broth was inoculated with the test organism
ii. Incubate at 37°C for 24 hours
iii. Add 0.5ml kovac's reagent through the sides of the test tube

4.5.3 Methyl red test

i. Inoculate the MR-VP (Methyl red-Voges-Proskauer) medium with the test organism
ii. Incubate at 35°C for 24 hours
iii. After incubation, add 3 drops of methyl red indicator and mix well

4.5.4 Voges-Proskauer test

i. Inoculate sterile MR-VP medium with test organism
ii. Incubate at 38°C for 24 hours
iii. After incubation, add equal volume of VP reagent I and VP reagent II and mix well

4.5.5 Citrate utilization test

i. Inoculate bacterial culture on Simmon's citrate agar slant with a sterile inoculation loop
ii. Incubate at 37°C for 24 hours

4.5.6 Triple sugar iron agar test

i. The triple sugar iron (TSI) agar slant is inoculated by means of stab and streak method
ii. Inoculate the isolates in the butt by using a straight needle
iii. The slant surface is then streaked following incubation determine the fermentative activities of the organism

4.5.7 Mannitol motility medium test

i. The medium is inoculated by stabbing the centre of the tubes to its base

    ii.   Incubate at $35 \pm 2°C$ for $18 - 24$ hours

4.5.8 Urease test
    i.   Inoculate urea agar with the test organism
    ii.   Incubate at $37°C$ for 24 hours

4.5.9 Nitrate reduction test
    i.   Streak the nutrient agar slant with test organism
    ii.   Incubate at $37°$ C for 24 hours
    iii.   Mix equal volume of reagent I and II in a test tube immediately before use
    iv.   Add 3 or 4 drops of the mixture to the culture

4.5.10 Catalase test
    i.   Place one drop of H_2O_2 on a clean glass slide
    ii.   Pick one colony from the solid media with the help of sterile applicator stick
    iii.   Place the colony in H_2O_2 taken on a slide

4.5.11 Oxidase test
    i.   Place the strip of filter paper on a clean petridish
    ii.   Add 2-3 drops of freshly prepared oxidase reagent
    iii.   The colony to be tested was picked with a sterile applicator stick and smeared over the oxidase paper

4.5.12 Coagulase test
    i.   Place a drop of physiological saline on both ends of the slide
    ii.   Emulsified a colony of the test organism in each of the drops to make thin suspension
    iii.   Add a drop of plasma to one of the suspension and mix gently
    iv.   Check for clumping of organism within 1 minute

4.6 Plant collection
The fresh leaves of *Justicia adhatoda* Linn. of acanthacea family were collected from the local areas of mulanthuruthy, district of Ernakulam, India.

4.7 Preparation of extract
500 gram of coarse powder of shade dried leaves of *Justicia adhatoda* was extracted with ethanol and keep three days for cold extraction. After three days filter the mixture using Whatman no1 filter paper. Ethanol was completely then evaporated by keeping it under water bath at $60°C$ to $80°C$. After complete evaporation of ethanol , the extracts were collected and stored in freezer at $-8°C$ for further dilutions and processing.

4.8 Antibacterial activity testing: agar well diffusion assay

- The selected organism were maintained in nutrient slants
- The organism were inoculated into peptone water and incubated at 37°C for 2 hours
- Prepare Muller Hinton Agar plates and agar wells were prepared with the help of sterilized cork borer with 10mm diameter
- The organism from the peptone broth were swabbed on the surface of sterile MHA plates using a sterile cotton swab
- Using a micropipette, different concentrations of the ethanolic extracts (20µl, 30µl, 40µl, 50µl and 60µl) were added to the wells in the plate
- Ethanol was used as negative control
- Ampicillin was used as positive control
- Plates were incubated in an upright position at 37°C for 24 hours
- The diameter of the inhibition zones was measured in mm and results were recorded

4.9 Phytochemical screening of *Justica adhatoda*

Phytochemical screening was done in order to detect the presence of bioactive constituents such as alkaloids , tannins , saponins , phenols , glycosides , flavonoids, etc using the methods described by Sofowora (1978), Trease and Evans (1989).

4.9.1 Test for saponins

2 ml of the ethanolic extract in a test tube was shaken for two minutes. Frothing which persisted on shaking was taken as evidence for the presence of saponins.

4.9.2 Test for alkaloids

3 ml of the ethanolic extracts was stirred with 5 ml of 1% HCl on a steam bath for twenty minutes. The solution obtained was cooled and filtered and to the filtrate add few drops of Mayer's reagent / picric acid . A cream precipitate indicates the presence of alkaloids.

4.9.3 Test for tannins

1 ml of freshly prepared 10% potassium hydroxide was added to 1ml of the ethanolic extract. The presence of a dirty white precipitate was taken as indication of tannins.

4.9.4 Test for flavonoids

To 3 ml of the ethanolic extract , a volume of 10% sodium hydroxide was added. A yellow coloration indicates the presence of flavonoids.

4.9.5 Test for phenolics

Two drops of 5 % ferric chloride were added to 5 ml of the ethanolic extract in a test tube. A greenish precipitate was taken as indication of phenolics.

4.10 Statistical analysis

The survey results were analysed and descriptive statistics were done using SPSS 12.0 (SPSS Inc., an IBM Company, Chicago, USA) and graphs were generated using Sigma Plot 7 (Systat Software Inc., Chicago, USA).

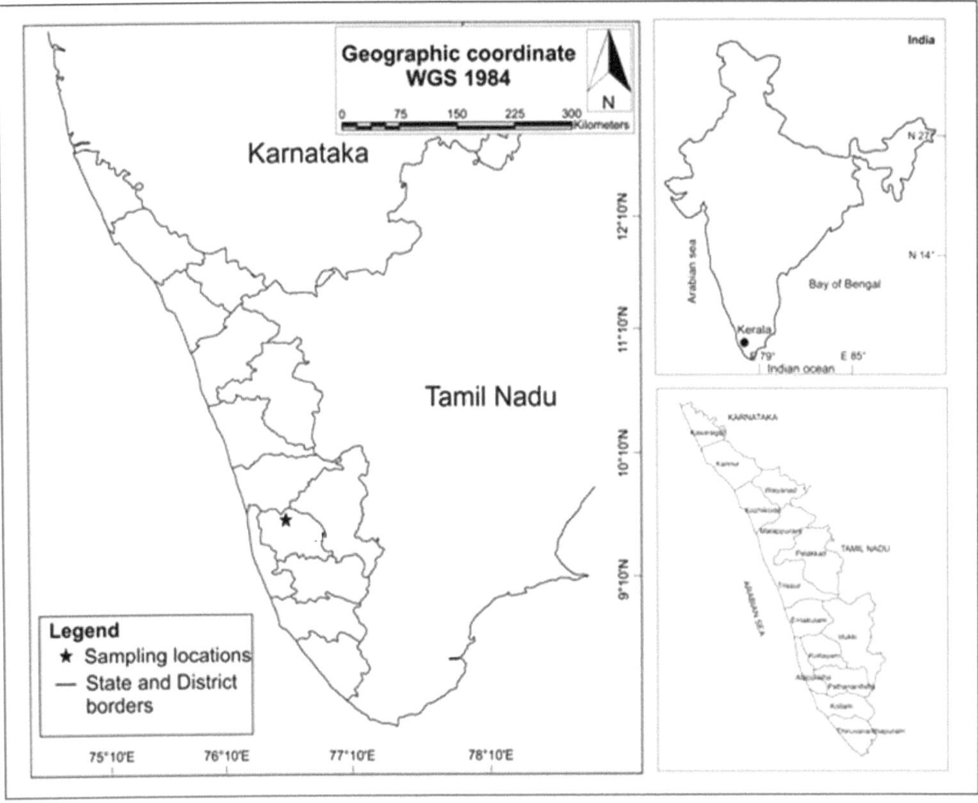

Figure 1. Map of Kerala showing the sample collection point. Authors own work.

Figure 2. Description of *Justicia adhatoda* a) plant with flowers, b) and d) mature leaves, c) plant with leaves and flowers. Photo courtesy: Wikipedia; Indiabiodiversity.org.

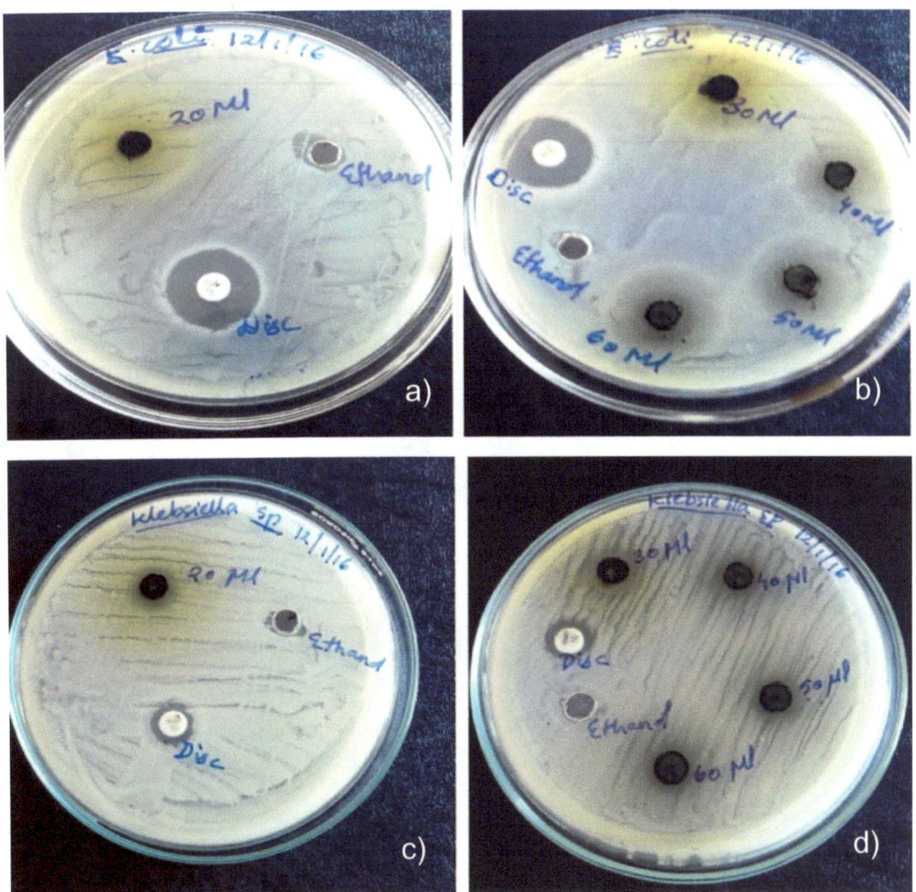

Figure 3. Antimicrobial activity of *Justicia adhatoda* a) and b) *Escherichia coli*, c) and d) Klebsiella species.

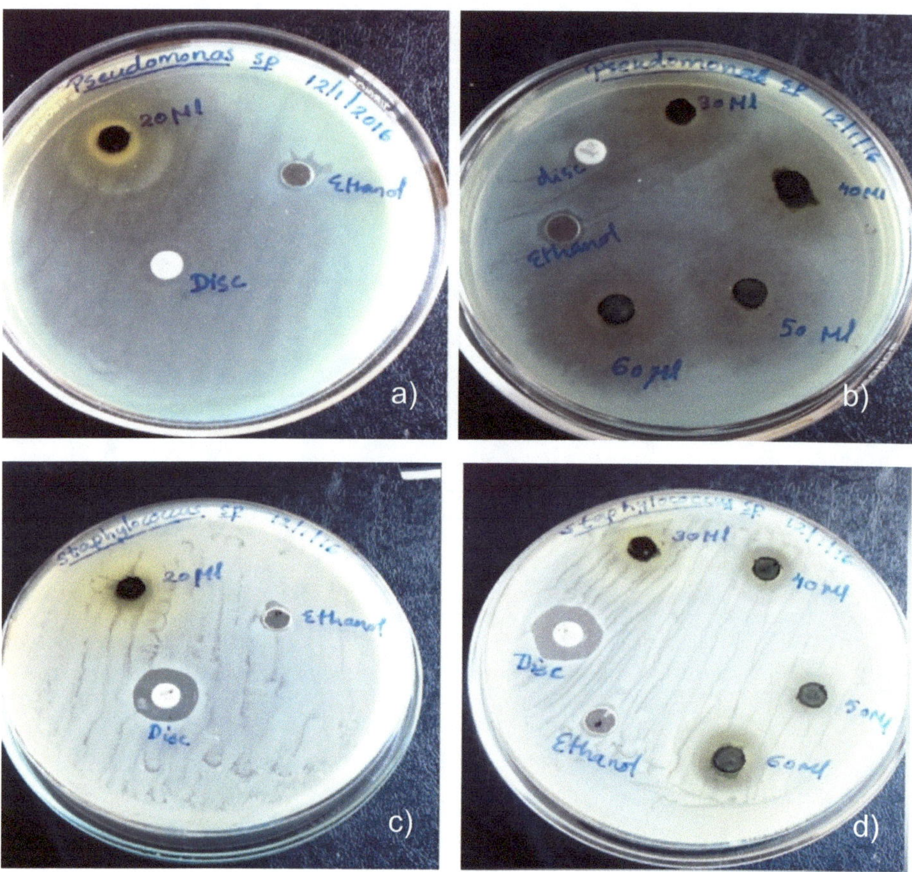

Figure 4. . Antimicrobial activity of *Justicia adhatoda* a) and b) Pseudomonas species, c) and d) *Staphylococcus aureus*.

Table 1. Colony morphology of the Isolate 1.

Medium	Size	Shape	Colour of organism	Margin	Elevation	Consistency	Opacity	LF	Haemolysis
Sterile nutrient agar	Small	Circular	colourless	Regular	Convex	Moist	Opaque	-	-
Sterile MacConkey agar	Small	Circular	colourless	Regular	Convex	Moist	Opaque	Yes	-
Sterile blood agar	Small	Circular	colourless	Regular	Convex	Moist	Opaque	-	No

Table 2. Colony morphology of the Isolate 2.

Medium	Size	Shape	Colour of organism	Margin	Elevation	Consistency	Opacity	LF	Haemolysis
Sterile nutrient agar	Large	Circular	colourless	Entire	Convex	Mucoid	Opaque	-	-
Sterile MacConkey agar	Large	Circular	colourless	Entire	Convex	Mucoid	Opaque	Yes	-
Sterile blood agar	Large	Circular	colourless	Entire	Convex	Mucoid	Opaque	-	No

17

Table 3. Colony morphology of the Isolate 3.

Medium	Size	Shape	Colour of organism	Margin	Elevation	Consistency	Opacity	LF	Haemolysis
Sterile nutrient agar	Small	Circular	colourless	Regular	Convex	Moist	Translucent	-	-
Sterile MacConkey agar	Small	Circular	colourless	Regular	Convex	Moist	Translucent	No	-
Sterile blood agar	Small	Circular	colourless	Regular	Flat	Moist	Translucent	-	Yes

Table 4. Colony morphology of the Isolate 4.

Medium	Size	Shape	Colour of organism	Margin	Elevation	Consistency	Opacity	LF	Haemolysis
Sterile nutrient agar	Small	Circular	colourless	Regular	Flat	Shiny	Opaque	-	-
Sterile MacConkey agar	Small	Circular	colourless	Regular	Flat	Shiny	Opaque	Yes	-
Sterile blood agar	Small	Circular	colourless	Regular	Flat	Shiny	Opaque	-	Yes

Table 5. Direct microscopic examination of isolated organisms.

Bacteria	Motility	Gram staining
Isolate 1	Motile rod	Gram negative
Isolate 2	Non motile rod	Gram negative
Isolate 3	Motile rod	Gram negative
Isolate 4	Non motile cocci	Gram positive

Table 6. Biochemical characterization of the isolated organism (Isolate 1).

Biochemical test	Observation
Sugar fermentation	
Glucose	Acid and gas
Lactose	Acid and gas
Sucrose	Acid and gas
Maltose	Acid and gas
Indole test	Red ring
Methyl red test	Red colour
Voges-Proskauer test	No red colour
Citrate test	No blue colour
TSI fermentation	
Slant	Acid (yellow)
Butt	Acid (yellow) and gas formation
H_2S	No H_2S production
Urease test	No pink colour
Mannitol motility test	Motile fermented
Catalase test	Effervescence
Oxidase test	No blue purple colour

Table 7. Biochemical characterization of the isolated organism (Isolate 2).

Biochemical test	Observation
Sugar fermentation	
Glucose	Acid and gas
Lactose	Acid and gas
Sucrose	Acid and gas
Maltose	Acid and gas
Indole test	No red ring
Methyl red test	No red colour
Voges-Proskauer test	Red colour
Citrate test	Blue colour
TSI fermentation	
Slant	Acid (yellow)
Butt	Acid (yellow) and gas formation
H_2S	Effervescence
Urease test	Pink colour
Mannitol motility test	Non motile, fermented
Catalase test	Effervescence
Oxidase test	No blue purple colour

Table 8. Biochemical characterization of the isolated organism (isolate 3).

Biochemical test	Observation
Sugar fermentation	
Glucose	No acid and gas
Lactose	No acid and gas
Sucrose	No acid and gas
Maltose	No acid and gas
Indole test	No red ring
Methyl red test	No red colour
Voges-Proskauer test	No red colour
Citrate test	Blue colour
TSI fermentation	
Slant	Alkaline (red)
Butt	Alkaline (red) and no gas formation
H_2S	No H_2S production
Urease test	Pink colour
Mannitol motility test	Motile, non-fermented
Catalase test	Effervescence
Oxidase test	Purple colour

Table 9. Biochemical characterization of the isolated organism (Isolate 4).

Biochemical test	Observation
Sugar fermentation	
Glucose	Acid only
Lactose	Acid only
Sucrose	Acid only
Maltose	Acid only
Indole test	No red ring
Methyl red test	Red colour
Voges-Proskauer test	Red colour
Citrate test	No blue colour
TSI fermentation	
Slant	Acid (yellow)
Butt	Acid (yellow) and no gas formation
H_2S	No H_2S production
Urease test	Pink colour
Mannitol motility test	Non motile, fermented
Catalase test	Effervescence
Oxidase test	No blue purple colour

Isolate 1 - *Escherichia coli*

Isolate 2 - *Klebsiella species*

Isolate 3 - *Pseudomonas species*

Isolate 4 – *Staphylococcus aureus*

Table 10. Antimicrobial activity of *Justicia adhatoda* against various bacterial isolates.

Bacteria	Inhibition zone diameter (mm)							
	Negative control	Positive control	20	30	40	50	60	
Escherichia coli	0	18	10	12	17	23	24	
Klebsiella species	0	16	11	16	15	17	18	
Pseudomonas species	0	7	23	26	28	30	30	
Staphylococcus aureus	0	11	13	13	14	14	14	

Table 11. Phytochemical activity of *Justicia adhatoda*.

Metabolite	Presence
Saponins	+
Alkaloids	+
Tannins	+
Flavonoids	+
Phenolics	-

5. Results and discussion

Plants are the important source of potentially useful structures for the development of new medicines. The growing population concern about health problems has recently led to the development of natural antimicrobials to control microbial diseases.

Antimicrobial activity of ethanolic extract of *Justicia adhatoda* were determined. Four organisms were tested (*Escherichia coli*, Klebsiella species, Pseudomonas species, *Staphylococcus aureus*). All organisms was sensitive against *Justica adhatoda*. The Pseudomonas species shows higher activity.

The mentioned organism may cause respiratory, skin, urinary and throat infection. *E.coli* may cause urinary tract infection. Pseudomonas species may cause throat and ear infection. Klebsiella species cause respiratory tract infection, wound and burn infections and nosocomial infections also. *Staphylococcus aureus* cause respiratory and central nervous system infections.

The comparison of antimicrobial activity of antibiotics and *Justicia adhatoda* against pathogenic bacteria reveals the potent antimicrobial activity of *Justicia adhatoda* .The *Justicia adhatoda* are more effective against the mentioned disease causing organism.

Emergence of multi drug resistance in human and animal pathogenic bacteria as well as undesirable side effects of certain antibiotics has triggered immense interest in the search of new antimicrobial drug of plant origin. The scientific study can serve as an important platform for the development of less expensive and effective medicine.

This study suggested that the less expensive , safe and effective natural extract of *Justicia adhatoda* are used instead of ampicillin antibiotic against the above mentioned disease causing microorganisms.

6. Conclusions

The selected plants contain potential antibacterial components that may be of great use for the development of pharmaceutical industries. The extracts possess significant inhibitory effects against tested pathogens. The above results open the possibility of finding new clinically effective antioxidant drug and could be useful in understanding the relationship between the traditional cures and current medicines. Further research is necessary to determine the identity of the antibacterial compounds from within these plants and also determine their full spectrum of efficacy. This study encourages the cultivation of this highly valuable medicinal plant to meet the increasing demand from traditional medicine system.

7. Future perspective

The present study of antibacterial and phytochemical activity of *Justicia adhaloda* revealed that effective ness of using this plant against various infections. These results could be used for the optimization of industrial and commercial production of the extract of *Justicia adhaloda*. Further studies are necessary for the detailed standardization of the antimicrobial activity of the extract against other potent pathogens.

References

Adnan, M., Hussain, J., Shah, M. T., Shinwari, Z. K., Ullah, F., Bahader, A., & Watanabe, T. (2010). Proximate and nutrient composition of medicinal plants of humid and sub-humid regions in North-west Pakistan. *Journal of Medicinal Plants Research*, 4(4), 339-345.

Agrawal, S., Chauhan, S., & Mathur, R. (1986). Antifertility effects of embelin in male rats. *Andrologia*, 18(2), 125-131.

Asolkar, L. V., Kakkar, K. K., & Chakra, O. J .(1992). Second Supplement to Glossary of Indian Medicinal Plants with active principles, Part I Publication and information Directorate (CSIR), New Delhi, India, pp. 78-84.

Atal, C. K. (1980). Chemistry and Pharmacology of vasicine: A new oxytocin and abortifacient. *Indian Drugs*, 15(1), 15-18.

Atta, U. R., Said, H. M., & Ahmad, V. U. (1986). Pakistan Encyclopaedia Planta Medica vol. I & II. Hamdard Foundation Press, Hamdard Centre, Karachi, Pakistan, 1, 51.

Ayyanar, M., & Ignacimuthu, S. (2008). Medicinal Uses and Pharmacological Actions of Five Commonly Used Indian Medicinal Plants: A Mini-Review. *Iranian Journal of Pharmacology and Therapeutics*, 7(1), 107-114.

Barry, V. C., Conalty, M. L., Rylance, H. J., & Smith, F. R. (1955). Antitubercular effect of an extract of *Adhatoda vasica*. *Nature*, 176(4472), 119.

Claeson, U. P., Malmfors, T., Wikman, G., & Bruhn, J. G. (2000). Adhatoda vasica: a critical review of ethnopharmacological and toxicological data. *Journal of Ethnopharmacology*, 72(1-2), 1-20.

Farnlof, A. (1998). Naturalakemedel and Naturmedel. Halsokas-Tradets Forlog. Stockholm, 109-132.

Jain SK (1991). Dictionary of Indian Folk medicine and Ethnobotany. Deep Publications, New Delhi, pp. 256-262.

Jain, S. K. (1965). Medicinal plant lore of the tribals of Bastar. *Economic Botany*, 19(3), 236-250.

Jain, S. P., & Puri, H. S. (1984). Ethnomedicinal plants of jaunsar-bawar hills, Uttar Pradesh, India. *Journal of Ethnopharmacology*, 12(2), 213-222.

Jain, S. P., Singh, S. C., & Puri, H. S. (1994). Medicinal plants of neterhat, Bihar, India.*I*, 32(1), 44-50.

Karthikeyan, A., Shanthi, V., & Nagasathaya, A. (2009). Preliminary phytochemical and antibacterial screening of crude extract of the leaf of *Adhatoda vasica*. L. *International Journal of Green Pharmacy*, 3(1), 78-80.

Kaur, R., Ruhil, S., Balhara, M., Dhankhar, S., & Chhillar, A. K. (2013). A review on Justicia adhatoda: A potential source of natural medicine. *African Journal of Plant Science*, 5(11), 620-627.

Kumar, A., Ram, J., Samarth, R. M., & Kumar, M. (2005). Modulatory influence of Adhatoda vasica Nees leaf extract against gamma irradiation in Swiss albino mice. *Phytomedicine*, 12(4), 285-293.

Lal, S. D., & Yadav, B. K. (1983). Folk medicines of kurukshetra district (Haryana), India. *Economic Botany*, 37(3), 299-305.

Maurya, S., & Singh, D. (2010). Quantitative analysis of total phenolic content in Adhatoda vasica Nees extracts. *International Journal of Pharmaceutical Technology and Research*, 2(4), 2403-2406.

Narimanian, M., Badalyan, M., Panosyan, V., Gabrielyan, E., Panossian, A., Wikman, G., & Wagner, H. (2005). Randomized trial of a fixed combination (KanJang®) of herbal extracts containing *Adhatoda vasica*, *Echinacea purpurea* and *Eleutherococcus senticosus* in patients with upper respiratory tract infections. *Phytomedicine*, 12(8), 539-547.

Nath, D., Sethi, N., Srivastava, S., Jain, A. K., & Srivastava, R. (1997). Survey on indigenous medicinal plants used for abortion in some districts of Uttar Pradesh. *Fitoterapia*, 68(3), 223-225.

Pandey, G. (2002). Anticancer herbal drugs of India with special reference to Ayurveda. Sri Satguru Publications.

Pushpangadan P, Nyman U, George V (1995). Glimpses of Indian Ethnopharmacology. Tropical Botanic Garden and Research Institute, Kerala, pp. 309-383.

Racle, J. P., Girard, M., Delage, J., & Constantin, B. (1976). Clinical and anatomopathologic effect of Bisolvon in respiratory resuscitation. In Annales de l'anesthesiologie francaise (Vol. 17, No. 1, pp. 51-58).

Rao, R. R., & Jamir, N. S. (1982). Ethnobotanical studies in Nagaland. I. Medicinal plants. *Economic Botany*, 36(2), 176-181.

Reddy, M. B., Reddy, K. R., & Reddy, M. N. (1988). A survey of medicinal plants of Chenchu tribes of Andhra Pradesh, India. *International Journal of Crude Drug Research*, 26(4), 189-196.

Roberts, E. (1931). Vegetable materia medica of India and Ceylon. Bishen Singh Mehendra Pal Singh.

Saralamp, P., Temsiririrkkul, R., & Clayton, T. (1996). Medical Plants in Thailand: Amarin Printing and Publishing Public Co. Ltd.: Bangkok, Thailand.

Sayeed, A., Madhukar, G., Maksood, A., Mhaveer, S., Athar, M. T., & Ansari, S. H. (2009). A phyto-pharmacological overview on *Adhatoda zeylanica* Medic. syn. A. vasica (Linn.) Nees. *Natural Product Radiance*, 8(5), 549-554.

Shah, N. C., & Joshi, M. C. (1971). An ethnobotanical study of the Kumaon region of India. *Economic Botany*, 25(4), 414-422.

Wren, R. C., Holmes, E. M., & Wren, R. W. (1950). Potter's cyclopedia of botanical drugs and preparations.

Krishnakumar, K. N., Rao, G. P., & Gopakumar, C. S. (2009). Rainfall trends in twentieth century over Kerala, India. *Atmospheric Environment*, 43(11), 1940-1944.

Appendix

MEDIA COMPOSITION

Nutrient agar

Peptone	: 0.5g
Sodium chloride	: 0.8g
Beef extract	: 0.15g
Yeast extract	: 0.15g
Agar	: 1.5g
Distilled water	: 100ml
pH	: 7.4 ± 0.2

MacConkey agar

Peptic digest of animal tissue	: 20g
Lactose	: 10g
Sodium tourocholate	: 5g
Neutral red	: 0.04g
Agar	: 20g
Distilled water	: 1000ml

Glucose phosphate medium

Peptone	: 5g
K_2HPO_4	: 5g
Distilled water	: 1000ml
pH	: 7.4 ± 0.2

Sugar fermentation media

Peptone	: 5g
Sodium chloride	: 20g
0.2% bromocresol purple	: 2.5g
Distilled water	: 1000ml

Tryptone broth

Tryptone	: 10g
Sodium chloride	: 5g
Distilled water	: 1000ml
pH	: 6.8 ± 0.2

Blood agar base

Protease peptone	: 15g
Liver extract	: 2.5g
Yeast extract	: 5g
NaCl	: 5g
Agar	: 15g
Distilled water	: 1000ml
pH	: 7.4 ± 0.2

Christensen's urea agar

Peptone	: 1g
Dextrose	: 1g
NaCl	: 5g
Monopotassium phosphate	: 2g
Agar	: 0.12g
Phenol red	: 15g
pH	: 6.8 ± 0.2

Simmons citrate agar

Sodium citrate	: 2g
NaCl	: 5g
K_2HPO_4	: 1g
$NH_4H_2PO_4$	: 1g
$MgSO_4$	: 0.2g
Bromothymol blue	: 0.08g
Agar	: 15.5g
Distilled water	: 1000ml
pH	: 6.8 ± 0.2

Triple sugar iron agar test

Peptone	: 10g
Yeast extract	: 3g
Beef extract	: 3g
Lactose	: 10g
Sucrose	: 10g
Dextrose	: 1g

Casein enzyme hydrolysate	: 10g
Sodium chloride	: 0.5g
Ferrous sulphate	: 0.2g
Sodium thiosulphate	: 0.3g
Phenol red	: 0.024g
Agar	: 12g
Distilled water	: 1000ml
pH	: 7.4 ± 0.2

Muller Hinton agar

Beef extract	: 30g
Casein hydrolysate	: 17.5g
Starch	: 1.5g
Distilled water	: 100ml
Agar	: 15g
pH	: 7.5 ± 0.2

Staining solutions

Gram staining

Crystal violet

Crystal violet	: 10g
100% ethanol	: 100ml
Distilled water	: 900ml

Gram's iodine

Iodine crystals	: 2g
Potassium iodide	: 1g
Distilled water	: 200ml

Safranin

Safranin	: 1g
Ethyl alcohol	: 40ml
Distilled water	: 300ml
pH	: 6.9 ± 0.2

Indicator solutions

Methyl red indicator

Methyl red	: 0.1g

Ethanol	: 300ml
Distilled water	: 100ml

Kovac's reagent

Butanol	: 150ml
p-dimethylaminobenzaldehyde	: 10g
Concentrated HCl	: 15ml

Oxidase reagent

Tetramethyl p-phenylenediaminedihydrochloride	: 0.1g
Distilled water	: 10ml

Voges-Proskauer reagent

Solution A	: 5% w/v solution
α-napthol	: 5g
Alcohol	: 100ml
Solution B	: 4% w/v solution
KOH	: 40g
Distilled water	: 100ml